Your Form Became My Own

Your Form Became My Own

Poems by

Jeanne Foster

© 2023 Jeanne Foster. All rights reserved.
This material may not be reproduced in any form, published,
reprinted, recorded, performed, broadcast,
rewritten or redistributed without
the explicit permission of Jeanne Foster.
All such actions are strictly prohibited by law.

Cover design by Shay Culligan
Cover art by Buford Mecklin Foster
"Two Birds" ceramic and wood

Author photograph by Alan Williamson

ISBN: 978-1-63980-233-3

Kelsay Books
502 South 1040 East, A-119
American Fork, Utah 84003
Kelsaybooks.com

For WJ

Acknowledgments

I am grateful to my mother, Buford Mecklin Foster, for leaving me her simple, graceful sculpture, "Two Birds," for the cover image. I also am grateful to my brother, Charles C. Foster, "Chuck," for helping me with some of the technical aspects of the production.

Special gratitude goes to my friend, Phyllis Stowell, who has stood by me and my work in times of discouragement as well as times of fulfillment. Along with Phyllis, I am thankful to the other members of our on-going poetry group, Sandra Gilbert, Peter Dale Scott, David Shattuck, Beverly Bie Brachic, and Katie Peterson, who have offered helpful comments on some of these poems. Most especially, I am grateful to one last member of the group, Alan Williamson, who has continued to love and support me through all the dreadful days of pandemic and to offer a positive look into the future. And finally, I'm grateful for the companionship of Dove Foster, my seventeen-year-old, golden, furry, feline beauty.

Thanks to the following:

The Closed Eye Open: "Iris, "Chilly Resolution"

Tennessee Williams Poetry Contest, New Orleans Literary Festival, finalist: "Two Nails," "Chilly Resolution," "Narrow Face"

Also by Jeanne Foster

Great Horned Owl
Poems

A Blessing of Safe Travel
Winner of the Quarterly Review of Literature Poetry Award
Poems

A Music of Grace:
The Sacred in Contemporary American Poetry
Critical Work

Appetite:
Food as Metaphor
Co-edited with Phyllis Stowell
Anthology of Women Poets

Goodbye, Silver Sister
Poems

The Living Theatre:
Selected Poems of Bianca Tarozzi
Co-translated with Alan Williamson
Winner of the Northern California Book Award for Poetry in Translation

Contents

ONE

Cut Rose	17
At Fiumicino	18
As We Lie Down to Sleep	19
Brenna	20
The Lizard's House	22
Your Charm	24
Meager Light	25
The Ancestors of this Place	26
The Air Redolent	27
The Racer	28
Taste by Taste	29
It Holds Still Here	30
Beetles	31
A Frame for Our Unreal	32
Here There Is Sound	33

TWO

Islands	37
Two Nails	38
Rat	39
Two Letters	40
Somewhere to Be Found	41
Here You Are the Window	42
Here You Are the Aged Cat	43
Here You Are Laid Out	44
Here You Are My Mentor	46
Here in the Romance of Evening	47
Here You Are the Addict	48
Brain Specialist Vet	49
Sea Drift	50

Alone on a Ridge	51
Reverse Vault of Sky	52
Wishbone	53
Narrow Face	54

THREE

Here You Are the Other Man	57
Marguerites	59
The Poise with Which You Leave	60
So Subtly You Insinuate Yourself	61
Chilly Resolution	62
Whole Trunks Have Tumbled	63

FOUR

Here You Are My Mother	67
Among the Constellations	68
Bare Bent Limbs	69
Letter Unsent to a Holy Ghost	71
Tunnels	74
Iris	75

Preface

These poems began as an address to a particular individual who has been in my life in one form or another for over twenty years. In an effort to understand the relationship, I discovered the particular *you* was ubiquitous, coloring everything in my life, merging, mutating, into other *yous* as divergent as lizard, cat, ocean, a dead friend, my mother, ultimately a spirit alive in the universe and in myself. It was very much as Eugenio Montale, another of my *yous,* says:

> *. . . I was permeated*
> *by you, your form became my own*
> *hidden breathing, your*
> *face melted into mine, and the obscure*
>
> *idea of God descended . . .*

Then I realized you are my creation as much as I am yours.

ONE

Cut Rose

Along the Roman wall,
you take my hand
for the first time
since the window
where I left the cut rose.
We walk with the young lovers,
our window of time
framed on the other side
by the timeless wall,
obscure, irregular
crannies and scrawls,
cracks that smell of the elements,
and we have no light,
but it continues.
The worn, burnt umber parallels
our parallel steps, well-placed,
that symmetry of stride our miracle.
Our considered walk.
Your arm is long, I remember.
Your fingers hang below mine,
interlaced, make the weight,
the weight of the thing, shift
lower, carried in a primitive place,
gulls caterwauling like unearthly toms
above the midnight roofs in the *centro*.
I ought not speak, I know, of
one creature, in and outside time
how we remain *unchanged together,*
for a year, a minute, an hour,
in love that can only burn.

At Fiumicino

Watching people disembark at Fiumicino,
you grouped me among the *scowly,*
as if I could choose to be
among the other *happy* half.
Sweet-smelling you, well-pressed, alert,
in your collar and red vest.
In the overnight flight's clothes, tunnel-faced,
I was afraid to look at you,
afraid to be seen outside my capsule
in the daylight, to be identified
in your too-bright eye by the lines
that make their pronouncement
upon my forehead:
she is one of the somber.

As We Lie Down to Sleep

As we lie down to sleep the world turns
half away . . .

                    You in your mother house
across the Tiber. I, with Elizabeth Bishop
in the bare-bulbed, heart of Rome pensione,
setting aside the poems, half a world away
from home, pad across the cool slab
to open the shutters.

                        The same woman is there.
I have seen her in both halves of the world,
in her rose-colored night dress
before the green screen,
typing, typing
the revolving night long.

Wondering what does it mean for the world
to turn half away, as you turn half toward
by day and fully away
by night from me?

Brenna

The wolf "Snow White"
and the one we call "Ugly"
because of his bulldog boxer
jowls—even more, his attitude—those two
yard mates behind the iron bar fence
a few handspans above our heads,
who snarl down as we pass up the steps
into the beamed kitchen
with quarried floor, have relaxed,

leaving us in silence, except for
an occasional rampage sparked
by a boy on bicycle or who knows what
shift in posture or tone of voice.
We sit in the scent of roses, on the *terrazza*
just outside the kitchen door—
at last, the peace we came for—corn rows,
rounded mountains, and the *bosco,*

where you can find the source
of the spring, the old woman in shawl
tells us *avanti* as we go to fill our bottle
from the village spout, the *bellisima* water
better than any bottled water, the chunk
of a man, balding, compact, sings to us
from his tractor *bellisima acqua.*

He guided us up from the pure river
where the road ends on the far side of Brenna,
when we lost ourselves and could not remember
the word for lost, guided us up
to *Casa Guerini,* our home for a while,

which has been our home already
for twenty-four hours and already
the dogs above us are quiet, for now.

River Merse, now we know where we are,
well-situated in our modest *bella* Tuscan town
that nobody ever heard of in the States,
south of Siena on the map,
at the end of a squiggly line
that peters out . . . sandy gold,
rushing over rocks into the filtered woods,
where the still water collects
and the trout.

The Lizard's House

This is the lizard's house—

who greets us the first day from the wide
storm drain outside the kitchen door: a curve
with star-toed feet, like the archaic letter "C"
with wings, that used to sing across the page
of my childhood alphabet book.

Dotted black and rare
spiritual yellow, though it is hard to say
which color forms the dots,
it disappears under the terracotta
flowerpot, lithe, cool
creature who inhabits our world
and lets *us* in. While we eat

pecorino and *pane* under the arbor
near the pink rose, the lizard
edges along the *terrazza* wall,
pausing now and then to lift its head toward us
in a curious salute. Its skin emits
a dewy glow as though
fresh from the shell.

One morning the lizard scurries across the tile
with a small one-of-its-own-kind held
in its thin smile. It heads for the storm drain
and the customary flowerpot:
a mother transporting her young, I think. Just then
the baby slithers free, maybe an inch in length.

It slides under a second flowerpot, a space
too narrow for the adult to follow. I glimpse
its preternaturally shortened tail.

We don't see the baby again, but our lizard
in its clean "C" more times than not
waits by the kitchen door to let us in—

a darkness that is brighter than ours.

Your Charm

Your stories always charm
my mother, and my father.
Unseasonable rain
taps on the patio roof
of a favorite trattoria,
the bamboo shades blowing in,
getting our feet wet.
Tonight, we three are charmed
out of our familiar *scowly*
constellation by the addition of
yourself; or, more rightly put,
we rose into ourselves—
the natural, easy-going selves
we can be with you
but alone together
cannot.

Meager Light

Another place another time—
you took me to the room
where you were born, spare,
unpainted wood, a single window,
meager light falling
on the bed. It had become

your sister's house. The second son
will be a priest, your mother
had ordained. You took me
over rain-logged grass to the church
you served as altar boy. The Celtic tower rose
giant in its midst. Alone,
in the bed where you were birthed, I stayed
the night.

The Ancestors of this Place

You open the little gate
and we step in
where all their eyes are bent on us,
rugged women and men,
the ancestors of this place, upright,
their photographs sealed upon the stones
on which their very names and fates
are engraved. We recognize

the keeper of the store where this morning
we bought our pecorino and bread,
the man on tractor who hailed us from the field
and told us only yesterday where to fill
our bottles with pure spring water.
We pass before each one,
searching, politely, for the eldest,
and when we find her
under a tender vine,
she has no photograph,
she is too old, and her stone
is broken off, leaving only the name,
Rose. All around our dry hill,

fields of sunflowers look as one
toward the sun of Tuscany.
We step into our shadows.
Before you leave, you take my hand.
Our separate thoughts lean like a single flower
toward the photographs of us.

The Air Redolent

The air redolent with cut flowers.
Every tomb has its bouquet.
How the people of the village down the hill
well remember you with colors, you
gone; do not seem to have been born
among the somber. Far back,

against the stone wall, in the single patch
of shade, one vase stands empty,
a piece broken from its side. Within
there is a glint, a movement.
A shining draws back and lies still,
hidden, almost, in a coil below the mossy green
two inches of rain, does not want to be known
by us who walk.

Sixteen years from now will you remember
this shining of the narrow face
as you remember today—ask me
to remember—the shining
rose of sixteen years ago?
You in your long bed will be too old,
though you say my name will be the last
upon your lips, to remember at all.

The Racer

Head like a shuttle stitching up and down the wall,
his bashful face wearing a horrified grin,
the long, long waist bent in a right angle, vertical
and horizontal over wall and walk,
the slapstick tail, all together

a stream of liquid muscle
no bigger around than your ring finger,
the racer gathers and slithers sidewise,
putting distance between him and us,

stumbling from parched olive grove and dry clods
upon the rear of the boarded up
rose-entangled, outgrown, stone, village
church, no bigger than your one-room school,
now his,

we two startled, quiet, as one
enchanted in earth's hour.

Taste by Taste

Half-lotus, in rose
light of candle. The hairs
on our bare knees, erect
intelligent feelers, measuring
the delicious space between
my left, your right.
How celibacy excites
the taste of death.

The way, standing by the hospital bed,
gripped by early, ingrown fear,
one feels one's hand hesitate
then taste by taste slip through
the sticky, putrid air
to take the dying hand one loves—
as if either touch or failing that
were death.

On our makeshift meditation cushions,
we gaze straight ahead, eyes half-focused,
toward the dresser's mid-section,
across the inch or less
that separates our knees
a shameless exchange.

Under the sheets, with a leg I sweep
the crisp, cool ecstasy of you
asleep on the sofa in the next room.

It Holds Still Here

Monte Oliveto Maggiore

The silence is green
as you lean back into the channel
your body cuts through air,
an existence tangible as beating wings
in rare moments of sunlight.
Down, down you go,
over nubby brick, among steadfast trunks.
Time is your friend because
it holds still here,
as though your hair were forever
just this shade.
Here your mother stokes the fire
with a lullaby on her rose lips.
Your father speaks a language
known to doves.
You whisper near my ear,
but I cannot understand the brogue.
You once thought the holy ghost
a faithful spirit. Then you knew it
hungry. Now you pause,
brush the tiniest particle of dust
from my cheek.

Beetles

Morning shimmers across even corn rows,
casts trapezoidal shadows on the forested hills
just the other side of this narrow valley.
Four black beetles, stocky, ugly fellows,
lodged in the leaves of the artichoke,
eat toward the heart.

On one of the terracotta roof tiles
conscripted to make a border for the artichoke
bed, an infant gecko appears,
scratches its side with its right front paw,
very like a warm-blooded soul,
then disappears under the curve of the tile.

Sounding like a giant popcorn popper,
the rock crusher in the far field,
a gangling, funny fellow we like to quip about,
circa the dawn of the Industrial Revolution,
starts up. You will leave for Rome today,
from the station in Siena.

A Frame for Our Unreal

Better not to analyze it, better not
puzzle away your powers. Isn't it
these connections across impossible space,
these beseechings, that give life
its meaning? On one side
the sunflower fields, on the other
the stiff climb up to the next level.
We drive in the shade of sycamores,
self-important through the dappling sun,
away from the memory of last night,
of the night long ago when we conceived,
odd blindness, our love—so quickly followed
by your *No . . . No . . .* and then *. . . No.*
And I must play it out one more time, making
the canopied green overhead—itself a richness
to dwell in—forever a frame for our unreal . . .
*Come with me, leave everything
and come with me . . .* but this time
the ghost of our future steps out
around the next gentle curve
of the road away from modest Brenna
and walks with a faintly rose-tinted hint
of the old allure directly toward us,
through us, into the past.
So, I am left on the leather couch
with a voice behind me
and myself.

Here There Is Sound

San Galgano

Here there is sound,
sound in fathoms
like ceaseless wind.
And if there is spirit,
spirit is
in the ruins of San Galgano,
gutted heart,
chamber of echoes,
great broken walls
and columns,
the ceiling sweeping strokes
of pure blue ether—
open soul.
Hear the quavering
from a thousand roosts.
Every cranny, nook,
the searing window holes
of the once rose,
now a pigeon's perch.
O hear without forgetting
the thousand echoes
of the thousand purple throats.
Spirito Santo
the common pigeon
dove of earth.

TWO

Islands

The Who . . . Who? of the train carries
in the purified air after rain
to houses, hearts, and automobiles parked
where romantics with no veranda
gaze toward the Golden Gate and remember
how the squall brought down the darkness
early to the Ligurian Bay of Poets,
where Shelley capsized and washed ashore,
and Byron cut his heart out
and preserved it,
                      and
lightning opened instants
above the hill we had navigated
reasonably well to arrive
at the Hotel Doria. Below our veranda
the town jabbered of the saint's feast day.
We went down for a meal
and the sky cracked with rain
and fireworks all at once.
That night you no longer with us
loomed in the fog mountain.
In sleep the storm blew across.
In the morning islands rose up from the sea
where they had not been the night before.

Two Nails

Two nails bleeding rust
rosacea at the peak
of a solitary salt-worn post.
They posture one to another
like giant sea weeds upon their long stems—
just that elegant drift of head.
Or like the mother on the beach
bent with concern toward the child. We are nailed

at the feet, always with this space,
this delirious atmosphere of sea between us,
and all around us an habitual beauty of the world
granted few. But we haven't arms to reach.
And so, we keen with our bodies, kept in place
while at the corner of the eye,
the prized silver
fish leaps.

Rat

Sausalito

Brazen rat, bitten of spine,
come out with the fat purple birds
to find a nub. Sewer rat,
driven by lack into the people's
light, clutching a crumb,
shivers only on the inside
as the athletic foot falls
a foot away, of the blond
who jogs past with a white parrot
balanced on her hand. You,

by your window in which this day
dies even as here it is born,
you through your rose-colored faith
would see only beauty
in a day that opens
like your lost wallet,
leaving to a stranger
your name, your money,
your credit, your license.

Two Letters

A letter comes from your side to my side.
At the eucharist each day, I think of you.
I was glad to be with you in Brenna.
I hope your new program goes well.
Tell your Mom and Dad hello,
will you? Remember the rose.

And then a letter comes
from your side to my side.
At the eucharist each day, I think of you.
I was glad to be with you in Brenna.
I hope your new program goes well.
Tell your Mom and Dad hello,
will you? Remember the rose.

I can nearly remember
this kind of forgetting.

Somewhere to Be Found

Are you in another form
somewhere to be found?
Your soul is old,
but not old enough
to have been enfleshed
in a body other than
the one I know.
At the nape of a neck
I feel the soft bristles
of hair. Not yours.
In the space sound carves out
for a voice, I hear
not yours.

I tried to force-bloom your death,
imagined—not having word from you—
that you had died in that sparse room
in the mother house,
and no one knew to tell me.
Then, *spirito santo,* you rose.
You were still alive.

Here You Are the Window

Mendocino

Here you are the window
and the flat flat roof
and the cove with its sable water
and the one, two, three, four,
five points of light on the far shore.
You are the ancestor,
wearing the slight frown.
To all the world it is judgment,
but you know it as your own.
Here the window is your frame.
In it things can happen.
For instance, a eucalyptus grove
where a pilgrim meets a master robed
in rose beside a sun-flecked
tombstone. Snap and aroma of dry leaves.
Actually, it is a painting in a box
across the mind. It could be replaced
by the sixteen or so baby graves
of mouse and gopher dropped by hawk,
each with its own engraved, wooden block.
Actually, that would be a painting
in a box across the gut,
bitty rodent tracks leading up
to the cavern heart, where a buoy sings
its most sorrowful song, in the mouse's ear,
in the box of the dead, in the window
of the room, in the frame of you.

Here You Are the Aged Cat

Here you are the aged cat
with blood in his stools.
I stay by his side,
saving you,
saving you
in your high cell room—
you wouldn't let me in—
overlooking Rome,
all the stone,
all the stones between us,
my imaginary child
whose feces I tenderly
collect, my imaginary
betrothed, tread softly,
Reverendo,
over red-tiled roofs
on my rose cloths.

Here You Are Laid Out

Here you are clean-washed and laid out
in white cotton on a high bed—
the small, black-and-white dog beneath,
expectant as we viewers come in,
quizzical tufts standing up under floppy ears.

You gaze from lowered lids,
I was going to say, languidly,
as though all the leisure of a Sunday morning
stretched out before you, or languid
as a slow-moving lagoon, but language
doesn't capture the eye beam,
the stroke of blue that arrests me
as I pass at your feet.
The horizon, they say, sometimes emits
a rare flash above the faceted sea
just at sunset.
We held our breath.

Sitting at your side, Zazen, the small dog
curled against my shins, I can see your chest
give a little rise and fall in silhouette
against the rice-paper shades, and suspect
you are still here after three cold days.

Your hands folded below the black bib
you sewed yourself when you took the precepts
that sustained you, the fingers rosy and warm
in the vault of that sunset at Asilomar—
betray you. Now, no color
beneath the nails, the pads
shrinking like an arid land.

Is it obscene to wonder about the flesh
that most betrayed you: the gland
so close to sex, so male? The devastation
it has wreaked within so limpid and thin
a body?

What does it look like?
More than the imagined,
the graphic vision might heal us,
your visitants, who can still think death—

if we are to be healed.

Here You Are My Mentor

Here you are my mentor
who speaks *wind
inthesailghostlove
Tillichsprucethreesand
dollarstalkingheads
somethingroseanything
youwanttodoanywhere
intheworldgoodJackDaniels
relationshipprivate
powerwheninIndia
somethingZenNo
impediment*.
I reach out to touch
and you are the intensest
shadow racing over
the mulled ochre beach,
startling me, only the etched angle
of wing, and you are gone.
I thought you were real.
Your odd ambiguity
seemed always to mean
something clear, if I had eyes,
ears. Fruitful.
Parable. Koan.
Did you stutter
as a child, or were you,
like Gandhi, simply shy?
You have turned the inarticulate
into a power I spend lives
trying to decipher.

Here in the Romance of Evening

Here in the romance of evening,
colored when I was twelve
on black construction paper,
eight-and-a-half by eleven,
full moon, staircase on the sea,
glistening palm trees, in Crayola,
yellow, flesh, and white . . .

it is you gliding over the expanse
of rose marble. Palm Beach, Florida.
Your lean strides, heel-toe, toe, toe-heel,
black tuxedo and I in my yellow feathers
gown, nothing will stop us now,
the seamless ballroom floor like satin
and forever dancing on the sea Fred Astaire
dancing the staircase to the moon
Shall we? dancing . . .

Here You Are the Addict

Here you are the addict
who walked across my floor
in stealth, who entered
by my bedroom window
and took the hummingbird
hovering above the rose, hand-painted
on the small round oval of wood,
you gave me on the Avenue of Giants
before you left,

who stole the promise
along with other keepsakes
and silver for cocaine,
of whom the policeman reassured,
*Don't be afraid. This kind of thief
does not come back,*
does not come back
like all men who break and enter
and do not return.

Brain Specialist Vet

The basilococcus is ubiquitous, the veterinarian says.
We don't know where it comes from;
it is found everywhere—positing the least of evils
to explain my honey-colored cat's sudden *grand mal* seizures.
We enter the darkened room. He flips the switch.
And in the frame upon the wall, a slice of skull,
a frontal view. *We're starting at the back,* he explains,
fanning through the layers of lit brain, slide by slide,
giving me a reading. From the corner of my eye,

I am surprised to see your Irish eyebrow hairs
in silhouette, on him—brain specialist
vet, giving me the bad news:
more likely a tumor, inoperable. A biopsy
is the only way to know for sure, and that means
drilling a hole through the skull.

Ubiquitous, you, my most constant recreation.

Sea Drift

San Francisco Bay

The feathery anise with succulent stems
is coming into blossom all along the unkempt
stone and sea drift shore—composite rock
and infernal plastic. The tassels of grasses,
the way they dip and lift in light wind, bring you
back to me. You, who never were,
might have been here,
any shore,
where somber I, where I
dream you up out of absence, that strange comfort,
out of longing, it is written:
her unquenchable thirst for disappointment.
An earthy sadness,
unearthly, it rises
from the pit which is the plague
of born Pisceans. The slip and fall
of the dancing master, the row
with the therapist, any death,
and your photograph emerges
from my black rose eye,
composite you, indestructible
as plastic, to be trusted
beyond warm blood and flesh.

Alone on a Ridge

On the distant rim of the coastal range,
a single, barely jade blip
on the otherwise sheet of grass green.
What a tree knows
standing on the backbone,
looking west, looking east,
isn't what you think,
isn't what you wish
as a gull flies through the beam
of your sight, that light current
not exactly longing.
To stand alone on a ridge
leaning vaguely to the wind
so as not to be blown off base.
In the letter that arrived today you write:
*my time in Rome is coming to a close,
new fellows will be put in my place,*
as though you want something of me
now that you are growing old
and being *put to pasture.*
All you have ever wanted of me
is dream, all—no matter the cut rose
or what I say—I have ever
wanted of you.

Reverse Vault of Sky

Your legions on liquid feet wheel upon the shore
to be pulled back into the lobed chamber,
reverse vault of sky, where you,
with all your returning souls, live.

One who walked our hill,
who knew by some sixth sense
the scent of our every neighbor's rose,
has returned home to you,
there, in that green wonderment.
And here on the kindled shore,
wishing almost to slip back
into your arms, I am closer to him

than the day we found each other
pressing against the same fence toward
the lilting face of the same rose—
scarred souls, burnt, like a brand
into the shoulder, longing for
this place where one slithers free
of the need for mind or feet.

You take and you take and you receive,
as when the newly ordained,
knowing little of your power or theirs,
give themselves over to your will.

This place where one slithers free
of the need for words or things.

Wishbone

Berkeley Y

You with ambition,
you with hard work,
who can accomplish any goal
(the fortune cookie says)—
concentrate on the valleys of the collarbones,
where the ends of the only wishbone
humans possess define the flesh.
As you walk out of your exercise sanctuary,
down the ramp for wheelchairs, into the old oil
parking garage—mercurial
rose-violet swirls—into the yellow ozone world,
hold in mind the softness of the valleys
either side of your neck,
a surrender much like prayer,
as much as we can know of that other valley
brightness of death.

Narrow Face

Calistoga

O narrow face,
hooded in black against the cold room,
O mouth, always vaguely open
to no purpose, neither to speak
nor eat nor cry out against the wretched
imbalance of the body tilted sidewise
chair-bound; O body situated before the window
by the too-kind giver of care, eyes that do not care
to see, O boat unable to right itself
sailing at an impossible angle upon the glassy river,
hung up by dammed sticks . . .

                             Morose familiar,
glimpsed by one outside the window, the stranger
passing in a car through a town visited before,
who turns around and passes by again
in the other direction, to be certain . . .
Yes, it is he: the now dead father.
It is you: the priest of her youth. It is she
in the hand of the one I am becoming.

THREE

Here You Are the Other Man

Villa Serbelloni

Italy, Italy . . .
I have my wish.
I sit on the castle rock, once was the rock
of Pliny the Younger.
The mist of evening flows into the mist of morning.
In this sky when am I waking,
when am I sleeping?
I try to imagine the shore watcher's house,
the one you say I do not remember,
the one you call the house of your evening.
I have tried to imagine it for years, more real,
really, to me than any house to stay in.
I am here where Pliny stood
and you have gone to the farthest continent.
So like you to write, *I'll be away,*
won't be able to see you, sweet rose,
I'm afraid, although the dates you quote
would leave you here in Italy
when I am. But I am—
Do I want to script this line?—
with another man. I *am.*
I told you I would be, and you replied,
having looked into your heart,
there is no ambivalence, I wish
you and Alain well. The bell.
It is noon. I have
a feather of a small bird between my fingers.
The tip is white, but for a minute tip
of midnight, of ink, distinct
the way such things are.
No meaning but in objects.
Here you are the other man.

Is it possible? Who wrote these words?
Here . . . and here . . .
You . . . and here . . . I'll do anything
to keep the mist from dissolving you.

Marguerites

These marguerites growing from the villa wall—
if you were here, we would stop
on the stone steps down to the village,
drawn as one to their small oxeyes.
We wouldn't speak.

You might speak, then, about
your brother, Christie, how he appreciated
small beauties. *Do you remember,
you would say, when Christie asked you,
"Do you know you are beautiful?"
And you replied, "Don't ask me. Tell me!"?*
Past the rose bushes and the fig trees,
we would take hands and walk as though
we had walked here yesterday
and would again. I feel safe
in your practised calm and want it to last.

I am walking down the villa steps
into Bellagio with another man,
clinging to your calm.
I am walking down the steps, pressed
between you and him—neither of you present—
unable to relinquish
a consummation that isn't to be.

The Poise with Which You Leave

Are you poisonous? So thin.
The angular markings
either side of your sleek head
raise the question.
And the poise with which you
leave, unhurriedly.
Stock still, I watch you wind
your way up the villa wall,
sliding over crevices large enough
for volunteer fig, phlox, rose to take hold,
glide unperturbed upon the world
of roots forced by the limited earth
into air, your brown-gold body
curving around the trunk
at the top and leaving
an idle question mark.

So Subtly You Insinuate Yourself

You catch us by surprise
so subtly you insinuate yourself
into our lives, crossing the sun's
late rose with angel's hair, blurring
the distant boundary of the sea,

and then at night, when we are asleep,
you begin your quiet tapping,
tapping into our brains, so that
we toss in liquid dream as you

sluice down roofs, drains,
the steep incline to Liguria,
where the fishing boat with its spotlight
turns in odd circles. We say

you weep, but of course
it is ourselves, wanting
not less than earth and sky
to sanctify our human project.

Chilly Resolution

Ligurian Sea

Your coast is rugged, thick
with rosemary and slide rock.
I want you to bring me to
your chilly resolution.
I want to know how it feels
simply to churn.
A shadow like a wheel,
but unmoved, unmoving
breaks the surface.
And you walk toward me,
your oddly formed toes
curving into a foot, the shape
of the Amati violin.
I make too much of my invention of you.
And then I make too much of it
that I have invented you.
The small, shedding eucalyptus,
where I sit, pushed more and more
to the edge by boulders fallen
how many years? Soon,
I will be back there
on the other side of the sea,
the only thing to show for the trip:
a savior with watery footprints.

Whole Trunks Have Tumbled

Behind the Ambrosiano Hotel in Milan
proper, a once-kept garden gone down.
Here we make our way around unwieldy rose canes,
over fallen branches. Whole trunks have tumbled.
In one quadrant, broken columns reminiscent of Pompeii,
but younger, one whose head rests against the cup of a giant,
Romanesque flowerpot. We sit on its slope, you the higher.
Two workmen, not in a hurry, tackle vines
with buzz saws; clearing the site, they tell us,
for another apartment building. You have traveled
all the way from Rome by train for this, although
you would not put it so. Overnight you have read
what I have written in this book:
Much of it very moving . . . Your voice trails off.
We are holding hands when you say you are *letting go*.
That cliché, in your Dublin baritone, is rendered true.
At home your young nephew had chided you: *"Uncle Bill,
why don't you remember?"* Without thinking, you replied:
"Because I'm seventy years old." You were
proud of that, you say, proud to be no longer
fighting age. I vacillate, as is my way,
between the old stance and the new—
but my heart isn't in the desire to win, win you from
the God I don't believe in. You kill me a little
when you say you wish me *and Alain well;
don't want to stand in the way;* then kiss me. A walk
through the early business hour to the underground.
As you go down, you turn around once.

FOUR

Here You Are My Mother

Here you are my mother, your too-bright eye

going blind, but slowly, along the successive
curve of time,
              reminding me,
of her fate in a single stroke: one eye blind—
                                        calling me,
though she is ashes gone
with sea and salt:

Do something!
Before it is too late! . . .

up against the gods, like the unenviable Greek,
trying to reverse destiny.

Among the Constellations

In the ambulance still in her black flats,
she kicks space, trying to make
room out there among the constellations,
kicking off the sheet with her red-pants leg,
setting free—even as I call her *Momma, Momma*
from the front seat, turning to reach,
and the driver says *You can't go back there.*
She doesn't hear you.

What I thought at first were raindrops
on the smallest branchings of the slender tree,
so pale it glows into the room even on the darkest night,
I now can see are buds, round as drops,
bulging with spring rains.
A tiny bird with a black cap,
very like my mother's favorite chickadee,
but with a lemon-yellow breast, lights there
for a sparkling instant, showering moisture to the earth
as it breaks an insect on the branch
or sharpens its beak against the silver bark.
Then flies away.

Surprising isn't it, how your tears are quieted
in a moment's attention to a small,
god-given other? You forget yourself.
Like leaves long at the bottom of the slow creek,
stirred up, rising to the surface:
a memory . . . or is it dream?
—*Did I kick the sheets all night,*
while lightning opened the meadow
and the olive trees? One blood one body? Here
you are she and you are not she,
painfully fearing you are.

Bare Bent Limbs

As morning slips over the oak and cypress forest,
a plane of light slices the early spring coolness,
beginning warmth falling against my face,
everything that would be green turned to blinding dew.
I am envious (You have well-taught me envy)
of your beauty and youth. We exchange places.

You are now where I have been in the light
that closes your eyes with its intensity.
And I am in your photograph.
You raise your arm and hand like a blade,
an almost salute, to shade your face,
and open your eyes toward a distant sound, an unknown bird?
there, across the river in its deep and slender bed,
there, from that far peak, who knows what odd cry
magnetizes you? and, through blood love, I hear.

Now I am in the light again watching morning awake
across the Chianti hills and meadows,
and you are back in the photograph
I carry with me everywhere in my mind.
Your wide stance, securely rooted to the earth,
trousers like sailor pants flaring at the bottom.
Your waist, proverbial hourglass, fluting upward
into slender rib cage, breasts.
Both arms raised now, you shield your face,
the wind catching some strands of hair,

one form, you and the sculptured tree
that stands behind you, all trunk
and bare bent limbs,
weathered and sleek of bone.
From where I am, you are both,

the one who has weathered years, now sitting in my chair
outside the cottage stone in Tuscany,
and the one whom I envy (also seated in my chair),
whom I know and have never known—
the sleek and silver you, enigmatic, twenty-six years old,
before you are my mother.

Letter Unsent to a Holy Ghost

You send me a copy of a book
a fellow priest wrote
How to Prepare for Death.
It is your manual.
You will do it correctly, practiced,
like your calm.

      ***

My mother,
whom I imagine as your sister—
I see her in your eyes—
all those years I kept you with me
though you were absent,
I was crying tears for her. My mother

blazed like an Independence Day flare,
then went out.
Went out without warning
just as my father, she, and I arrived
at the Holiday Inn, Navarre Beach,
the Gulf Coast of her youth, everyone there,
the celebration of their sixtieth anniversary,
she in her red suit, her silken hair
waving about her face
gently . . . gently . . .

      ***

That night in Milan,
the final time you were with us,
my family of three,
her eyes shone with that special blue,

though one was already blind
from what they call a "stroke of the eye."
You couldn't tell which one.
She flung the brilliant orange-and-rose
scarf around her neck and over her shoulder,
as we stepped out to dinner.
Hand-embroidered raw silk from Como,
I had chosen it, knowing her flair for color.
The scarf, along with your presence,
seemed to drive away what haunted her.
My father's doggedness relaxed too.
She and I, even he, we all three loved you.

    ***

Years before you had given me
what they say all children need,
even the child in the adult.
Fromm coined it unconditional love.
I called it re-mothering.
You believed in God's love
and I believed in you.
Your blue eyes, straight nose,
high cheek bones, and pointed chin
convinced me you were her kin,
and a second mother to me.
You were my father's brother too
(in Uncle Max, I saw you), and yet
you were a father to my father.

    ***

Did my mother know that day, before her mirror
as she dressed to go? She put on
the pendant—the one I gave her—

pewter with an inlay of red stone.
At the rest stop, only two hours
before the beginning of her death,
she and I alone:
You have on the pendant I gave you.
It's perfect with that suit. I didn't know you ever
wore it. And she, in a sweet and steady voice,
perfectly pure but, like a chime, a sound with no
clear edges: *I like it. I wear it all the time.*
Still ringing. Why didn't I say to her
the words I longed to hear?

I didn't know.
We were heading for the Gulf of Mexico
and the hotel on the dunes she loved.
She went out in her red suit, left her guests
with nothing. All loose ends, no good-byes,
no announcements she was "letting go."
Left declaring she was in *good shape.*
But did she know? In the bell of her voice
wasn't there something especially sweet and true?

      ***

We have become one: she, you, I, in my mind.
Now, we are dying all over again.
When she and I were alone that last time,
weren't her words her way of saying,
My daughter, I love you?

The only answer I know is the answer I invent.

Tunnels

The Dolomites

The malaise descends,
a dank mist that penetrates
the spaces of my brain . . . the nausea spreads
upward from the solar plexus,
pressing on my heart . . .
my body falling into trance,
as though willed from somewhere else . . .

I enter the caverns of pitch and dolomite,
my slight vehicle pinned behind and in front
by carbon-dioxide belching hulks,
on my left two-eyed meteors—sudden, fading lights—whiz by,
close on my right, the wall of chiseled mountain stone . . .
cold stone that would break a moving body
into smoldering, fuming, bleeding, parts . . .

Unfocusing eyes, I order you to focus
on that yellow globe fanning before me
into the blackness . . . Breath, I say, breathe . . .
hypnotist, clap me awake . . .

And I break out into daylight . . .

My answer is to dare
you, tunnels,
to risk the body
to avoid the wreckage of the soul.

Iris

*Only this iris can I
leave you as testimony
of a faith that was much disputed,
of a hope that burned more slowly
than a hard log in the fireplace.*

. . . a history endures in ashes alone . . .
                    —Eugenio Montale

Following a night of brilliants,
Orion and the seven sisters, I awake
to frosty overcast and hurting vision.
It is true what you say: this iris
is the only testimony, and its witness
is doomed. The closing each night
is a signal.

           That one oak leaf
alone—among the others
that have held on all winter
warming the hills with rusty color—
takes up batting the air like a beguiling wing.
And nothing else moves.
It is true what you say about memory.
Ashes . . . ashes . . .

And what's that you say about faith?
A little book. A few words transcribed.
A hair. A single strand. At dawn
the opening eye
that burns with dust,
still opening.

About the Author

Jeanne Foster is Professor Emerita at Saint Mary's College of California. She also is a Unitarian Universalist minister. Born in Florida, she grew up in New Orleans and graduated with Honors from Tulane University. On a Woodrow Wilson scholarship, she studied with acclaimed process philosopher, Charles Hartshorne, and German Heideggerian, Karsten Harries, at the University of Texas in Austin. It was after she moved to Boston that she began to focus on creative writing at the Boston School for Adult Education. At Breadloaf Writers' Conference, she worked with Galway Kinnell and, while there, was persuaded to spend some time in Buffalo, where John Logan invited her to sit-in on his writing workshop. He also introduced her to James Wright, visiting one summer at the University of Buffalo, who became her primary mentor and a friend. From Buffalo she took a wide leap across the continent to Berkeley, where she received an M.Div. degree followed by a Ph.D. in Religion, Literature, and the Arts from the Graduate Theological Union. After six years as pastor in Modesto, she opted for a teaching career at Saint Mary's. She has published widely in journals, including *Hudson Review, Paris Review, The Nation, Narrative,* and *APR*. Her early poetry collection, *A Blessing of Safe Travel,* won the Quarterly Review of Literature Poetry Award. Of a later collection, *Goodbye, Silver Sister,* Richard Tillinghast writes: Foster "makes a reader feel he is entering deep into what Yeats called 'the labyrinth of another's being.'" On sabbatical in Italy, she had the good fortune to meet Bianca Tarozzi, Professor Emerita, the University of Verona, who translated a portion of this later book into Italian for *Poesia*. Foster is co-translator with Alan Williamson of *The Living Theatre: Selected Poems of Bianca Tarozzi,* which won the Northern California Book Award for Poetry in Translation. She has received grants from New York State Creative Artists Public Service Foundation, MacDowell, Saint Lawrence and Lannan Foundations and was Poet-in-Residence at Tulane University. Her passion is ballroom dancing, and, in particular, ballroom dancing in Tuscany.

www.ingramcontent.com/pod-product-compliance
Lightning Source LLC
Chambersburg PA
CBHW030913170426
43193CB00009BA/828